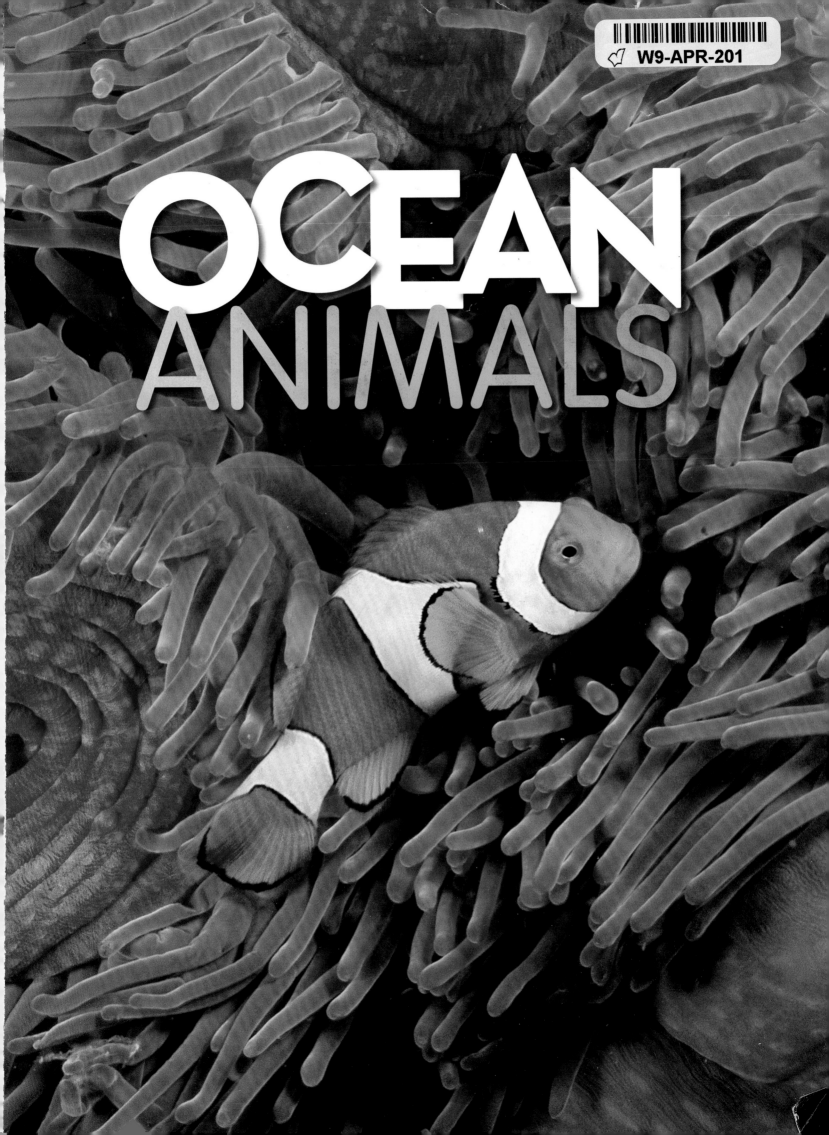

OCEAN
ANIMALS

OCEAN ANIMALS

WHO'S **WHO** IN THE **DEEP BLUE**

JOHNNA RIZZO

WITH AN INTRODUCTION BY SYLVIA EARLE

NATIONAL GEOGRAPHIC
WASHINGTON, D.C.

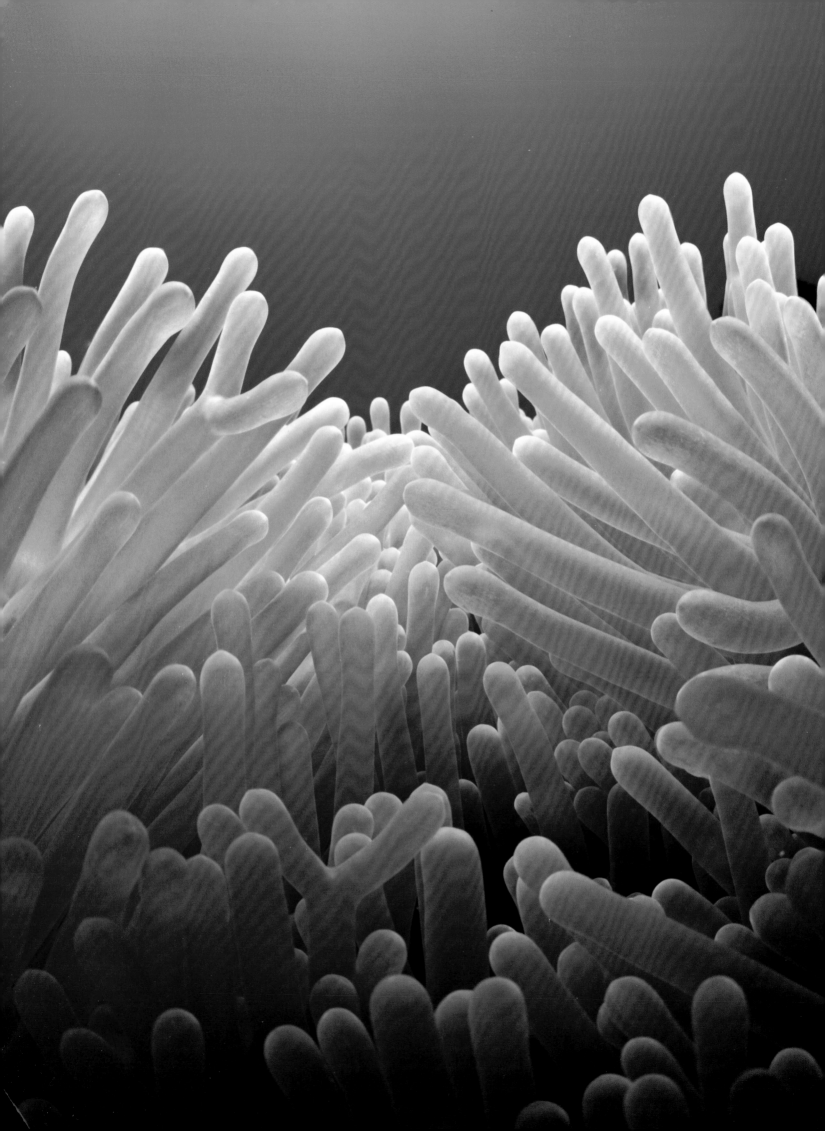

TABLE OF CONTENTS

A lionfish swims over the Tubbataha Reef in the Philippines.

⟡ INTRODUCTION

Imagine what it must be like to be a dolphin, living in a realm of liquid space, listening to the whistles and clicks of nearby family members. Have you ever wondered what it's like to be a jellyfish, with 99 percent of your body made of water? Or how about a clam, hunkered down in a soft, sandy bottom, sipping plankton-filled water through a special tube, rather like drinking soup through a straw? Imagine living in the deep sea, beyond the reach of the sun's rays, lighting your way with the flash, sparkle, and glow emitted from your own body. As a marine biologist and undersea explorer, I have spent thousands of hours in the ocean, getting to know some of the millions of kinds of plants, animals, and other life-forms that live there—far more than exist on the land. It is obvious why all of these creatures need the ocean. It's their home!

But what about us? We now know that the ocean gives Earth an oxygen-rich atmosphere that makes it possible for land animals (including us) to live. It steadies the temperature, drives climate and weather, and yields fresh water to the sky that returns to

Adélie penguins leap from an iceberg.

the land and sea as rain, sleet, and snow. There can be water without life, but nowhere is there life without water, and 97 percent of Earth's water is in the ocean.

Like life in the sea, we need the ocean, and now the ocean needs us. Pollution, overfishing, and other things people have done to the sea are causing problems that dolphins, jellyfish, and clams can't solve. The good news is that humans can, and it starts with understanding the nature of the ocean—and knowing why it matters. This book is a wonderful place to begin.

SYLVIA EARLE

OCEANS
OF THE WORLD

National Geographic recognizes one world ocean. To simplify things, most geographers divide it into four oceans: Pacific, Atlantic, Indian, and Arctic.

PACIFIC

The biggest ocean on Earth, the Pacific hugs the planet nearly halfway around and contains almost half its ocean water. Stretching along the west coast of North and South America all the way to the east coast of Asia, the Pacific contains some 25,000 islands. It is also home to Challenger Deep—the deepest place on Earth and the lowest point in the Mariana Trench.

ATLANTIC

The saltiest ocean of all, the Atlantic stretches from the east coast of North and South America to the west coast of Europe and Africa. In the frigid northern part, near Greenland, five-story-tall icebergs loom. Deep below the surface, about halfway between Europe and the Americas, lies the Mid-Atlantic Ridge, the longest mountain range on Earth. It's as long as the Andes, Rockies, and Himalaya combined.

INDIAN

Formed more than 65 million years ago when present-day Africa separated from Antarctica, India, and Australia, this is the youngest of all the oceans. It curves around the southern coast of Asia and stretches from the east coast of Africa to the west coast of Australia. Powerful winds, called monsoons, blow from the southwest between May and October and from the northeast between November and April.

ARCTIC

Wrapped around the North Pole, the Arctic is the coldest of the oceans. It is so far north that the sun barely rises for much of the winter. Pack ice drifts in frigid currents, colliding and refreezing—creating a partial ice cover that can be more than a hundred feet (30 m) thick in some places. For a few months in the summer, the sun shines almost 24 hours a day, melting some of this ice. Also the smallest and shallowest ocean, the Arctic is almost completely closed off by the northern borders of North America, Europe, and Asia.

a FIFTH OCEAN?

The Atlantic, Indian, and Pacific Oceans meet up around the continent of Antarctica. Some experts call this the Antarctic, Austral, or Southern Ocean. But is it really a separate ocean? Some say no, that it's just a place where three oceans meet. Others say yes, because the water has distinct currents and temperatures.

LAYERS
OF LIFE

At the ocean's greatest depths, the seafloor is almost seven miles (11 km) below the water's surface. Under the waves, even in places where the sun never shines, beautiful and strange life-forms find ways to thrive.

tropical fish

the SUNLIGHT zone

From the ocean's surface to about 328 feet (100 m) below the waves, plants, plankton, and animals soak up the abundant sunlight that filters down from above. Sea creatures big and small feast in this nourishing underwater garden.

the TWILIGHT zone

Very little sunlight reaches the twilight zone, between about 328 (100 m) and 3,300 feet (1,006 m) deep. No plants can survive here. Only specifically adapted living things, such as jellyfish and bacteria, flourish this deep. Fish, squid, and shrimp travel between the sunlight and twilight zones in search of food. Sperm whales search for squid at this level in hopes of scoring a tasty meal. But these animals all return to the sunlight zone before long.

squid

the MIDNIGHT zone

anglerfish

Dropping from roughly 3,300 feet (1,006 m) to the ocean's deepest trench, almost 36,000 feet (10,973 m) down, the midnight zone encompasses some three-quarters of the ocean, where the temperature hovers near a frigid 39°F (4°C) and light rays fade away. To survive, deep-sea creatures have adapted strange ways to hunt and scavenge for food (see pages 94–97).

1. blue shark
2. common dolphin
3. yellow sea horse
4. blue-girdled angelfish
5. clown triggerfish
6. moonfish
7. flyingfish
8. green sea turtle
9. comb jellyfish
10. sunfish
11. Portuguese man-of-war
12. humpback whale
13. harbor porpoise
14. common eagle ray
15. jellyfish
16. bluefin tuna
17. Pacific giant octopus
18. plankton
19. deep-sea squid
20. viperfish
21. lanternfish
22. deep-sea glass squid
23. bell jelly
24. hatchetfish
25. sperm whale
26. dragonfish
27. giant squid
28. rattail fish
29. deep-sea zooplankton
30. snipe eel
31. vampire octopus
32. siphonophore
33. black seadevil
34. black swallower
35. antimora
36. smoothhead
37. anglerfish
38. gulper eel
39. fangtooth
40. amphipod
41. crown jellyfish
42. decapod
43. barreleye fish
44. deep-sea zooplankton
45. tripodfish
46. giant sea spider
47. glass sponge
48. snailfish
49. deep-sea cucumber
50. brittle star

ILLUSTRATION NOT TO SCALE

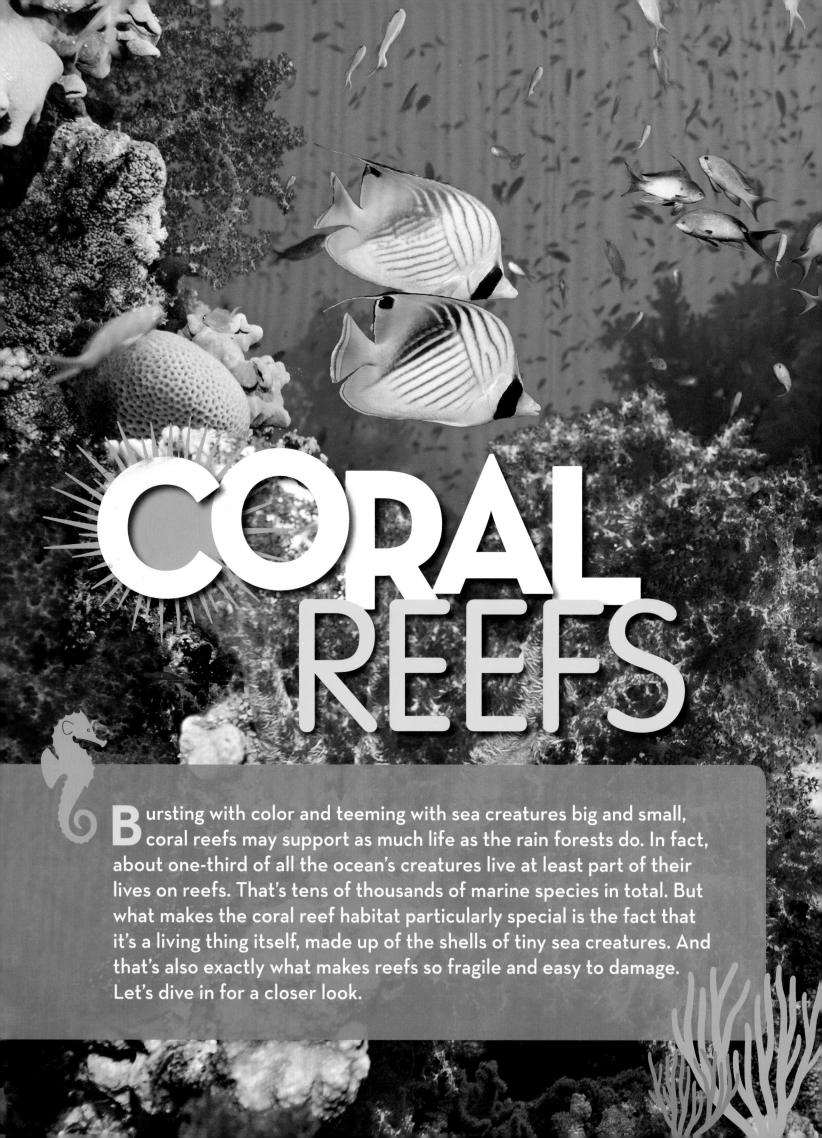

CORAL REEFS

Bursting with color and teeming with sea creatures big and small, coral reefs may support as much life as the rain forests do. In fact, about one-third of all the ocean's creatures live at least part of their lives on reefs. That's tens of thousands of marine species in total. But what makes the coral reef habitat particularly special is the fact that it's a living thing itself, made up of the shells of tiny sea creatures. And that's also exactly what makes reefs so fragile and easy to damage. Let's dive in for a closer look.

Golden and threadfin butterflyfish search for polyps and worms on a coral reef in Egypt's Red Sea.

Some **coral reefs** on Earth today **began growing** more than **50 million** years ago.

Fish swim over soft corals in Fiji.

animal ARCHITECTURE

These reefs may look like a pile of pretty rocks, but corals are actually groups of tiny animals called polyps. Polyps are soft organisms that build limestone shells for protection. When the polyp dies, its hard shell remains. In the ocean's warmest waters—about 70°F (21°C) is the perfect temperature—these tiny polyps build shells one on top of the other, creating stony reefs of monumental size over thousands of years.

house of a
DIFFERENT
COLOR

Using the sun's light, brightly colored algae grow in the polyps' soft tissue, producing some of the itty-bitty animals' food and giving each coral its distinctive color. Without these algae, polyps would turn white and die. Different species of coral (there's 2,300 kinds in the world!) have many varied shapes that look like everything from elks' horns to organ pipes to human brains.

collared butterflyfish

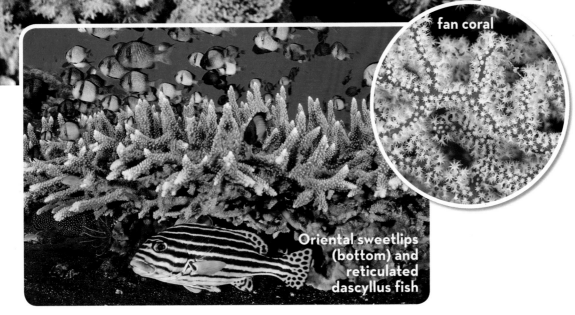

fan coral

Oriental sweetlips (bottom) and reticulated dascyllus fish

look out: VENOM AHEAD!

textile cone snail

Among the creatures that flit, float, and frolic among the colorful corals are some of Earth's most venomous. And there's not just one method of imparting a serious sting. Sea anemones, close cousins of coral and jellyfish, use their bright colors to camouflage reef-friendly clownfish and can also unleash their tentacles for a deadly sting when other species of fish swim by. Pretty seashells on the ocean floor can also be deadly. Textile cone snails—among the world's most toxic creatures—chomp down on prey with hollow teeth, through which they inject lethal venom. They've even been known to munch on their own species when food is hard to find.

A clownfish hides from predators in a sea anemone.

sea anemones
seen up close

LARGEST CORAL REEF
in the world

Australia's Great Barrier Reef stretches some 1,250 miles (2,000 km) and is one of the largest natural structures on Earth. Longer than the Great Wall of China, it can even be seen from space! More than six hundred islands and thousands of smaller coral reefs link up like a massive chain running parallel to Australia's northeast shoreline. In this sun-drenched part of the ocean, it's possible to see as far as 100 feet (30 m) down into the brilliant blue water. The sun's rays create a welcoming home for at least 300 species of hard coral, 4,000 species of mollusks, and 1,500 species of fish that swim throughout the reef.

The Whitsunday Islands sit in the Great Barrier Reef off the coast of Australia.

sweetlips fish

box jellyfish

fish on the Great Barrier Reef

clownfish

a rainbow of
REEF LIFE

Thousands of animal species take refuge in coral reefs around the world. The unique and colorful creatures shown here, and many others, depend on the reef environment for food. They also camouflage themselves in its candy colors.

four-striped damselfish

angelfish

parrotfish

blue tang

lionfish

Moorish idol

sea anemone

mandarin fish

yellowmouth moray eel

SEAHORSES

fin FLOURISH

Fluttering 35 times each second, small fins on a seahorse's back propel this tiny animal upright through the water. Two tiny fins on its head help steer as its curled tail unfurls and trails behind. In fact, a seahorse's fins never, ever stop moving. To stay in one place, a seahorse uses its tail to grab onto sea grass or coral. All that scooting around takes a lot of energy. These ravenous carnivores have to eat almost constantly to stay alive, gulping up to 3,000 tiny brine shrimp every day, as well as other small animals and algae. Their long snouts suck up these tasty treats.

Always on the **lookout** for predators, a seahorse can **move** its **eyes** in **opposite** directions at the **same** time.

Japanese seahorse and babies

daddy DUTY

Seahorses are among only a few animal species on Earth in which the male carries the young before birth. The female seahorse places a hundred or more eggs in a pouch on the male's belly. The male fertilizes the eggs and carries them around in his pouch. About a month later, the father seahorse opens the pouch and gently pushes out the tiny babies. The young fend for themselves from the moment they are born.

leafy sea dragon

thorny seahorse

SEAHORSE VS. SEA DRAGON

A seahorse's closest relative is the leafy-limbed sea dragon. Here's the secret to telling these look-alikes apart.

SEAHORSE:

- swims vertically
- can grab objects with its tail
- eggs are kept in the male's pouch
- no fleshy appendages

SEA DRAGON:

- swims horizontally
- tail is not used as an anchor
- eggs are attached to the male's tail
- has fleshy appendages for camouflage

Atlantic seahorse

SEA URCHINS

home SECURITY

Sea urchins come with built-in predator protection—making it tougher for crabs, eels, birds, and sea otters to make them their next meal. Some are armored in long thin spikes; others live inside a hard shell, but that's not always enough to keep them safe. They also have clawlike structures (called pedicellarines) that can sting, And some, like the fire urchin, have venom on the tip of their movable spine. These adaptations aren't just to keep them alive, though. Their spines help them move, working in tandem with five paired rows of tiny tube feet with suckers on the end. Cousins of sea stars, sea urchins also see by detecting light through their spines.

The **red sea urchin** lives **longer** than **any other** animal. Many of them reach **more** than **200 years old.**

wolf eel eating a red sea urchin

mouth of a fire sea urchin

CHEW on this

Sea urchins are omnivorous, munching on both algae and coral, as well as dead fish, sponges, and barnacles. Their spines and the suckers on their feet help them trap food particles floating by in the water. They also forage among sea rocks. In fact, researchers recently found that the sound of sea urchins' teeth scraping on reefs can contribute to a rise in ocean noise!

purple sea urchin

SEA STARS

Sea stars use sea water instead of **blood** to pump **nutrients** through their **arms.**

sea star in the Galápagos Islands

arm CHARM

Arms are extremely important to sea stars. Rows of tiny tube feet line their undersurface, creating suction to help sea stars crawl along the ocean floor. Their vital organs are located in their arms, and their eyes—or rather eye spots—are on the tips. They help the animals detect light. Sea stars have at least five arms, but some species can have as many as 40. If any of them get bitten or broken off, special cells migrate to the injury site and begin to regrow the appendage.

underside of a sea star

Some sea star species can **extend** and **retract** their **gill structures**—the **fuzzy-looking** stuff on top of their **bodies**—through their **skin**.

sea stars clinging to a rock

stupendous STOMACH

There are as many as 2,000 species of sea stars, and almost all of them have a different diet. These cool creatures eat everything from bivalves, barnacles, crabs, and fish to plankton, sea anemones, and even other sea stars. But more than *what* a sea star eats, it's pretty amazing *how* it eats: It grips prey with its water-filled tube feet, then brings its stomach outside its body. It surrounds the food, then uses a special fluid to digest it. When the sea star is finished with a meal, it brings its stomach back inside its body. Now that's eating out!

common sea stars

a sea star that looks like an octopus

blue sea star

CRUSTACEANS

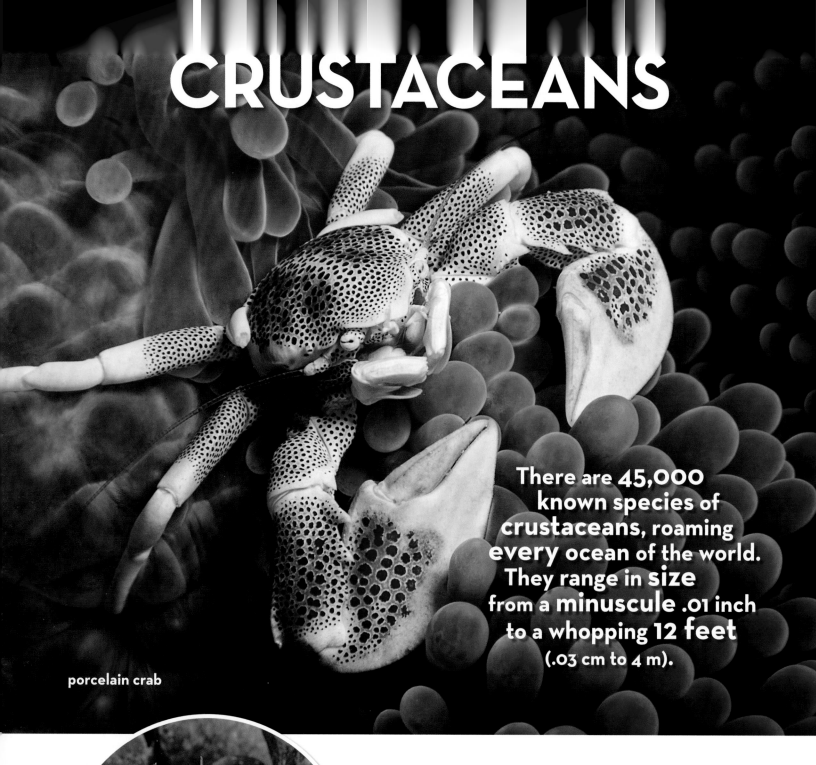

There are **45,000** known species of **crustaceans**, roaming **every** ocean of the world. They range in **size** from a **minuscule** .01 inch to a whopping **12 feet** (.03 cm to 4 m).

porcelain crab

hard-core HOUSING

Crustaceans are built for self-protection. Popular snacks for sea otters, hammerhead sharks, and hundreds of other sea animals, some of these crawlers hide by digging holes in the squishy mud. But crabs, lobsters, shrimp, and other crustaceans carry their most important line of defense on their backs: hard shells, or carapaces, that make the animals difficult to swallow and challenging to chew. As crustaceans grow, they molt, shedding their old shells and growing new ones that fit better. The swap happens as often as once a month for fast-growing young crustaceans.

European lobster

shelled
SCAVENGERS

Scuttling along on jointed legs, pincers constantly picking at the rocks and sand in a quest for food, crustaceans generally aren't picky about what they eat. They'll nibble everything from plants to other crustaceans to dead animals. Many of these scavengers have antennae above their mouth and a pair of claws just below their mouth that they use to grab prey. Some crustaceans, such as lobsters, have a larger claw on one side that comes in handy for crushing shells, and a smaller claw on the other side that is perfect for picking out the meat.

Hawaiian lobster

spotted cleaner shrimp

superior shells,
TAKE 2

Crustaceans aren't the only group that has perfected the shelled life under the sea. Many mollusks have amazing shells, too! Instead of molting like crustaceans, though, many mollusks keep building their shells over their entire lives. Scallops, clams, and oysters are familiar mollusks that might appear on the dinner table, but there are actually about 100,000 different species of mollusks. Ranging in size from smaller than an inch (2.5 cm) to more than 26 feet (8 m), many of these soft-bodied animals have shells. Others, such as octopuses and squid, are shell free. Small mollusks are fast food for predators such as sea stars, sea otters, crabs, and many other sea creatures.

giant clam

OCEAN EXTREMES

wild wonders

Earth's crust, or hard surface, is separated into colossal sections called tectonic plates, which are in constant motion, bumping and scraping against each other. Volcanic eruptions and mountain and crevice creations are some of the extreme results of all the commotion in the ocean.

A stack of **25 Empire State Buildings** could fit inside the Mariana Trench.

deepest trench

Some of the oceans' deepest, darkest secrets lie in a 35,827-foot (10,972-m) abyss called Challenger Deep, which lies at the bottom of the Mariana Trench.

Located smack in the center of the Pacific Ocean, the deepest place on Earth has been visited by only three people. What's down there in the inky blackness is still one of the world's biggest mysteries.

hydrothermal vent in the Pacific Ocean

hottest habitats

Deep below the ocean's surface, frigid seawater seeps into cracks in the seafloor, trickling into Earth's crust. There, the heat from molten rock, or magma, heats the liquid until a boiling, black mixture of water and minerals burps back out, creating a hydrothermal vent that reaches up to 752°F (400°C). Over time, the minerals collect and form tall structures called chimneys that attract strange sea creatures, such as 6-foot (1.8-m)-tall tube worms and blind shrimp.

longest
mountain range

You can't hike to the top of these peaks—they're a mile under the sea! The world's longest mountain range, called the Mid-Atlantic Ridge, stretches some 6,214 miles (10,000 km) down the middle of the Atlantic Ocean—more than twice the distance from Washington, D.C., to Los Angeles, California.

fissure zone caused by the Mid-Atlantic Ridge

biggest explosions

Thousands of active volcanoes are percolating under the sea. When they blow, they sometimes spew steam, smoke, lava, gas, and ash hundreds of feet into the air. If an underwater volcano erupts again and again over millions of years, hardened lava collects and forms new islands. The U.S. state of Hawaii is actually a volcanic island chain.

undersea volcano exploding near Tonga

OCTOPUSES

an octopus swimming in the sunlight zone of the ocean

cloak of
INVISIBILITY

Slinking along the sandy sea bottom, lurking and watching—octopuses are underwater spies, always on the lookout for a crab or lobster to devour or predators to avoid, such as sharks and other large fish. When they do spot attackers, they protect themselves with escape tactics worthy of a secret agent. Their skin is filled with chromatophores—groups of special cells filled with different colors—which spread out and turn an octopus's skin the same color as its surroundings. The sly creature then becomes virtually invisible as it skirts rocks and crevices.

Pacific giant octopus spraying ink

supersonic and stealthy
ESCAPE SYSTEM

An octopus crawls slowly while hunting, but when it becomes the hunted, look out! It can perform the ultimate vanishing act. Shooting out a cloud of black ink, the animal confuses its stalker. At the same time, the octopus juts its eight legs straight behind it, squirts water from deep inside its body, and uses jet propulsion to quickly dart away.

Though adult octopuses range from 0.5 inch (1.3 cm) to 20 feet (6 m) long, all newborn octopuses are the size of a pea.

an octopus swimming in the deep ocean

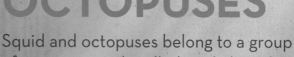

SQUID VS. OCTOPUSES

Squid and octopuses belong to a group of marine animals called cephalopods. But these cousins have a number of differences.

SQUID:

- most have eight arms and two tentacles
- generally lays its eggs and leaves them
- has hooks or rings on its suckers

OCTOPUS:

- most have eight arms and no tentacles
- generally protects its eggs until they hatch
- has only suckers

squid

JELLYFISH

feats of EATING

See-through, squishy, and mostly blind, jellyfish bob along with the rhythm of the waves and currents. Tiny, venomous cells on tentacles stun shrimp, fish, and other small sea creatures that swim across a jelly's path. Jellies then use their tentacles to haul them in. Since they don't have digestive tracts, these blobby creatures use their stomach juices to liquefy prey.

One of the **most interesting things** about these **gelatinous creatures** is that **they don't have brains.**

A group of jellyfish is called a bloom, swarm, or smack.

mighty MORPHER

sea nettle jellyfish

Emerging from its egg, a young jellyfish soon becomes a polyp, or a small cylinder-shaped creature with a mouth at its top surrounded by tiny tentacles. It attaches itself to something in the sea, such as a rock or coral. Eventually, it turns into a tiny jelly called an ephyra, with an umbrella-shaped body and swinging, swaying tentacles. The ephyra is tiny—about a millimeter wide. But don't let their small size fool you. Most young jellies will chow down on plankton almost nonstop until they become adult jellies, called medusas. While jelly stings can be deadly to some sea creatures, for others, such as sea turtles and some fish, jellies make a wonderful meal.

luminous jellyfish

Nomura's jellyfish

jumbo JELLYFISH

Growing from the length of a grain of rice to the size of a washing machine in just six months, Nomura's jellyfish are some of the largest in the world. Found along the coasts of China and North and South Korea, each giant jelly weighs some 450 pounds (204 kg).

37

SHARKS & RAYS

The ocean is full of fish species, and none cause a sense of awe and wonder like sharks. Some scientists also consider rays to be flat sharks. Either way, there's an underwater world of variety—and a whole lot of eating—going on in the ray and shark families. Have a look inside the watery world of these apex predators.

A great white shark disrupts a school of fish near Guadalupe Island, Mexico.

SHARKS

blacktip shark

undeniable TOP DOG

A great white shark—which can weigh as much as ten gorillas—detects splashing near the ocean's surface. After accelerating, the powerful predator smashes through the surface, grabbing a desperately flapping seal. Then, flipping head over tail, the shark slams against the water. Great whites never chew their meals. Instead, they rip them into chunks and swallow. They swallow smaller prey whole.

the MEAL DEAL

Sleek and silent, sharks prowl through the watery depths, stalking fish, seals, squid, and other sea creatures. In the eat-or-be-eaten world of the ocean, sharks almost always come out on top. With sharp vision, muscular bodies, and the ability to smell blood from a great distance, sharks are designed to hunt. Before a shark even sees a fish, it can detect its heartbeat through electric sensory receptors. These tiny, gel-filled canals in the shark's snout, called the ampullae of Lorenzini, let the hunter know when prey may be hiding nearby. Once this stealthy predator has settled on its supper, it speeds through the water to catch its prey. A shark's skin is designed to reduce the water's drag on its body, so some sharks can cruise up to 20 miles an hour (32 km/h).

great white shark

who EATS whom

PREDATOR ⟶ PREY

GREAT WHITE ⟶ mostly seals, sea lions, and fish

TIGER SHARK ⟶ anything, including other sharks

WHALE SHARK ⟶ mostly plankton, some squid and fish

HAMMERHEAD, NURSE, LONGNOSE SAWSHARK ⟶ crabs, shrimp, squid, and fish

Longnose sawshark
Length: up to 5 feet (1.5 m)
Weird but True: The teeth of a baby longnose sawshark are folded back until it's born so it doesn't scratch its mom's body.

face-to-face
WITH SHARKS

The top of the food chain and the biggest fish in the sea, a shark weeds out weak members of other species and prevents overpopulation. Sharks may seem scary, but they often get a bad rap. Only about four fatal shark attacks on humans occur each year—humans are actually a much greater threat to sharks. There are 460 species of sharks that range from 6 inches (15 cm) to 40 feet (12 m) long. Get up close and personal with some of these powerful predators.

Lemon shark
Length: 8 to 10 feet (2.4 to 3 m)
Weird but True: When flipped onto their backs, lemon shark babies become naturally paralyzed for several minutes—a state called tonic immobility.

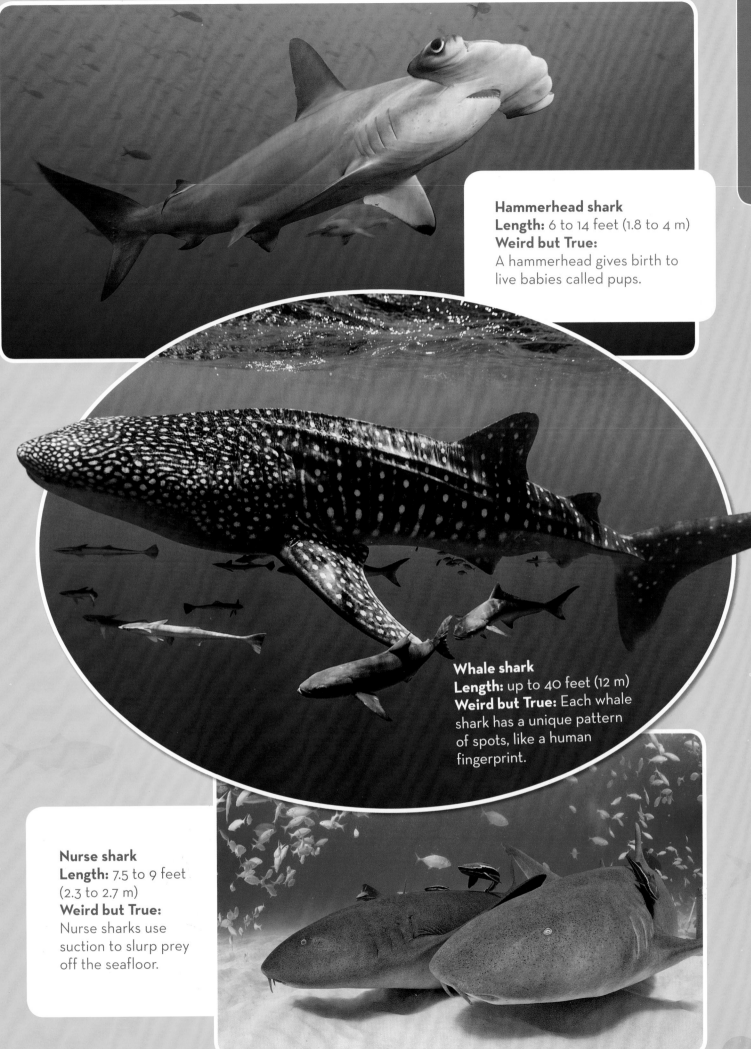

Hammerhead shark
Length: 6 to 14 feet (1.8 to 4 m)
Weird but True:
A hammerhead gives birth to live babies called pups.

Whale shark
Length: up to 40 feet (12 m)
Weird but True: Each whale shark has a unique pattern of spots, like a human fingerprint.

Nurse shark
Length: 7.5 to 9 feet (2.3 to 2.7 m)
Weird but True: Nurse sharks use suction to slurp prey off the seafloor.

RAYS

underwater
BALLET

Rays often rest on the ocean floor, safely camouflaged like a rock in the sand, and come out only when it's time to hunt for a seafood dinner. A ray swims with a rhythmic rise and fall of its side fins, almost like a bird flapping its wings. A few up-and-down movements are enough to keep its diamond-shaped body gliding through the ocean. Rays look weightless in the water, but the biggest species, the 2,000-pound (907-kg) manta ray, actually weighs about as much as a cow. As it moves, gill slits on its underbelly absorb life-giving oxygen from the water.

eagle rays in the Maldives

southern stingray resting on the sandy ocean floor

sharp and SHOCKING

When provoked, some rays, called stingrays, use their whip-like tails as powerful weapons of self-defense. With lightning speed, a ray can lash an attacker with the saw-edged, stinging spines on its tail, inflicting serious pain. Electric rays have real shock value. When hungry or threatened, two kidney-shaped electric organs in their bodies send out jolts of up to 200 volts—enough to power a hair dryer—to kill prey, and to keep hungry sharks and orcas away.

feeding FRENZY

First a few manta rays arrive, then suddenly there are hundreds. Mouths open, round and gaping, a group of mantas swims through a tasty mass of plankton and krill. As they feed, the mantas form an orderly line. This is called chain feeding. When 50 or more mantas start chain feeding, something amazing happens. The head of the line catches up with the end, and the rays swirl around and around, creating a manta cyclone. When more than a hundred mantas join the group, the spiral breaks apart. A free-for-all begins, with rays bumping into each other as they wolf down their tasty meals.

southern stingray gliding through the water

manta rays feeding on plankton

MARINE MAMMALS

It might seem odd that some animals who call the oceans home need to breathe air. More than that, a lot of them also sleep, relax, and have their babies above the surface. But it's in the oceans where these marine mammals hunt and eat—crucial parts of an animal's survival. Discover why these air-breathers are so attached to the oceans.

Both male and female walruses have tusks that can grow to about three feet (1 m).

WALRUSES

Staying **warm** is a **team effort** for these **social** animals. **Hundreds of walruses pile** on **top** of **each other**, their **blubbery** bodies keeping each other **cozy.**

massive MEALS

Snout down in the sandy seafloor, a walrus sweeps its face back and forth, using its whiskers to scrounge for clams. In seconds, the walrus swallows one down and spits out the shell. These giants polish off hundreds of pounds of shellfish every day to keep their 3,700-pound (1,678-kg) bodies moving through the ocean. When a walrus is done with its underwater feast, it swishes its tail to push its massive body up through the water. Face poking through the surface for a breath, the walrus spurts water to clean out its whiskers.

SEA LION VS. WALRUS

Seals (including sea lions) and walruses make up a family of marine mammals called pinnipeds, which have flipperlike limbs. Find out some of the differences between sea lions and their walrus relatives.

SEA LION:

- does not have tusks
- front flippers propel it through water
- has ear flaps on the outside
- has 40 to 60 whiskers
- is up to 11 feet (3 m) long

WALRUS:

- has tusks
- hind flippers propel it through water; front flippers steer
- has internal ears
- has 400 to 700 whiskers
- is up to 12 feet (4 m) long

sea lion

walrus

not-so-graceful
ICE DWELLERS

Using its three-foot (1-m)-long tusks to haul itself onto the Arctic ice for a rest, a walrus rotates its strong flippers under its body and then raises its body up for a look around. But the animal is anything but graceful when it walks on land, clumsily flopping along like a gigantic inchworm. Walruses spend half of their time feeding in the water, and the other half lounging and living on the ice, so they have to migrate to stay with their habitat. They follow the sea ice north when it melts in the summer, and then head south in the winter when the ice returns.

A group of walruses is called a herd.

SEA OTTERS

A sea otter's teeth are 2.5 times stronger than human teeth.

excellent
TABLE MANNERS

Floating belly up, their backs cradled in the ocean water, sea otters don't even flip over to eat. Instead—CRUNCH!—they use rocks to crush clamshells and open spiky sea urchins. Using their tummies as tables while they snack, sea otters wash their bellies after every meal so food doesn't get stuck in their very thick fur.

northern
sea otter

a **HAIRY** situation

Whether they live in mild or cold climates, sea otters have up to a million hairs on every inch of skin—the densest fur of any animal. This double layer of fur traps air bubbles next to their skin, which helps keep sea otters warm and helps them float. After diving under the waves, a sea otter blows air back into its fur with its mouth. Sometimes it does somersaults to force air inside its dense coat. A sea otter's thick fur also helps newborns bob along on the water with their mothers.

sea otter floating in kelp

sea otter in **Monterey Bay, California**

A sea otter floats solo in the frigid waters off the coast of Alaska.

in good—and protective—COMPANY

In a behavior called rafting, sea otters sometimes gather in groups to socialize, to rest, and to watch out for each other. If one sea otter perks up, the others suddenly pay attention, too. When orcas and other predators, such as eagles, sea lions, or sharks, are nearby, the otters scatter into the water, darting away to safety.

a raft of northern sea otters

sea otters in Prince William Sound, Alaska

mother sea otter and newborn pup

Mama otters most often **carry** their **babies** on their **tummies** and even **nurse** them as they **float** on their **backs.**

MANATEES

Manatee calves stay with their mother for one to two years.

Florida manatee

West Indian manatee

West Indian manatee eating some leaves

gentle GIANTS

Some early explorers spied manatees with seaweed draped over their bodies and mistook them for mermaids. In reality, they look more like sumo wrestlers. Sometimes called sea cows, full-grown manatees weigh in at a whopping 800 to 1,300 pounds (363 to 590 kg) and can eat as much as a tenth of their own body weight in sea grasses and other plants every day.

life in the
SLOW LANE

Flicking their strong, paddle-shaped tails, manatees glide along at a leisurely five miles an hour (8 km/h)—so slowly that algae can actually cling to their soft, wrinkly skin. But these marine mammals can ratchet up to speeds of 20 miles an hour (32 km/h) when necessary. Living in warm, shallow waters, manatees use their front flippers to steer, sticking their snouts above the water's surface every 10 to 25 minutes to breathe.

The **manatee's** closest **relative** on **land** is the **elephant.**

POLAR BEARS

Polar bears live in the **Arctic**, an **area** made up of the Arctic Ocean and **some land**, with **lots** of **ice** cover at the **northernmost** part of **Earth**.

a mother polar bear and her cub walking along the ice

fur FACTS

Polar bears blend into their snowy, icy environment perfectly—but their fur isn't actually white, it's transparent. Each strand's hollow center scatters light and makes a polar bear's coat look white. Their skin, on the other hand, is black, which helps soak up all the sun's rays. Underneath, a layer of fat four inches (10 cm) thick keeps them toasty and helps them float when they're in the water. Matted, dirty fur wouldn't keep them warm on land, so polar bears are all about keeping clean. After a meal, they'll dip into the water and then wipe themselves clean in the snow for a full 15 minutes. Sometimes, they slither through the snow to get their tummies spick-and-span, or roll on their backs to get the parts they can't reach with their paws.

paw
POWER

polar bear in Canada

Polar bears move slowly and steadily across the slippery ice, in large part because their huge paws—up to 12 inches (31 cm) across—help distribute their weight evenly. These unique paws are covered with tiny bumps, called papillae, which act like treads. Fur also sprouts between the bears' toes to help keep them on their feet even in the slipperiest of situations. Their two-inch (5-cm)-long claws—perfect for catching and holding their seal prey—also help grip the ice. In the water, those paws, which are slightly webbed, turn into paddles, helping the bears slice through the current. Their front paws pull them through the water like oars, and the hind paws help them steer.

polar bear swimming in the frigid waters of the Arctic

OCEAN EXTREMES

into the unknown

Humans know more about the surface of the moon than they do about the bottom of the ocean. Like outer space, Earth's oceans are an unfriendly environment for human survival. The deeper you travel, the more intense the water pressure becomes. Without protection, the human skull and bones would be crushed, and veins and arteries would collapse. Plus, extremely cold temperatures (above and below the surface) could be life-threatening. Extreme machines like the ones described here help scientists stay safe while they explore the ocean.

biologists working in an ice bucket

ice BUCKETS

A massive ship called an icebreaker crashes through the iceberg-filled polar waters. Slowing to a halt, the ship extends a crane-like arm that lowers explorers onto nearby ice in a people-size bucket. Scientists examine the frozen terrain, gathering information from these dangerously cold and icy regions. Then the bucket lifts them to safety back aboard the warm ship.

super SUBS

Submersibles, or submarine-like diving machines, are built to withstand the massive pressure of the deep ocean. Scientists maneuver through the water, taking along lights, cameras, and recording equipment to help them document what they see. One of the most famous submersibles, called *Alvin*, can journey as deep as 4,764 feet (1,452 m) and has made more than 4,400 dives.

Sylvia Earle in the JIM suit

diving SUIT

The JIM suit—which controls pressure and temperature—helped oceanographer Sylvia Earle make the deepest ocean dive ever to 1,250 feet (381 m) below the water's surface.

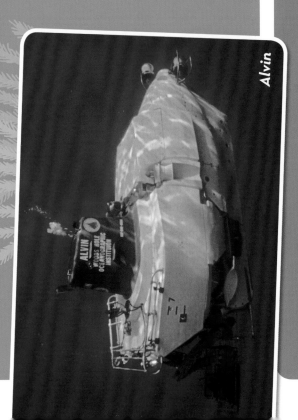

Alvin

undersea ROBOTS

Remotely operated vehicles, or ROVs, can journey as deep as 2,400 feet (732 m). A scientist on a ship uses a joystick to steer a robot through areas too dangerous for humans. Connected to a ship with cables, an ROV has robotic arms that delicately pluck samples from the seafloor. This new generation of unmanned vehicles is helping bring the mysteries of the sea to the surface.

underwater robot

WHALES & DOLPHINS

With sleek skin built for diving deep and slicing through waves at high speeds, dolphins and whales are superb swimmers. But these animals are also master communicators, creating songs and systems of clicks and chirps to let one another know what's going on under the waves. Take a look at the world of these amazing ocean mammals.

Spotted dolphins ride the waves in Hawaii.

WHALES

a lot of HOT AIR

All whales are mammals that must surface regularly to breathe in air through their blowholes. The ocean water parts as the whale splits the surface, blasting a gigantic spray into the air. But this isn't the only dramatic view one can catch of whales. Humpback whales and other species of marine mammals leap out of the ocean belly up and arch their backs as they plunge headfirst under the waves. This impressive leap, called breaching, lasts only a few seconds. Scientists think it might be a form of communication.

humpback whale breaching

ocean COMMOTION

Like their dolphin cousins, whales can be pretty mouthy mammals. A blue whale's underwater call is as loud as a jet engine, but the tone is too low for humans to hear. Of all whales, humpbacks have some of the longest and most varied songs, crooning for up to 15 minutes at a time. What these songs mean is one of the great mysteries of the sea. Only male humpbacks and blue whales are known to sing, but many species have calls, ranging from barks to chirps to moans, screams, and pops. Some scientists think the songs attract females, or just announce to other males, "I'm here."

krill swarm

Antarctic krill

big beast, LITTLE FOOD

There are two groups of whale species: baleen and toothed. Baleen whales such as blue whales, right whales, and humpbacks are toothless filter feeders. With mouths open wide, they take in gallons of water along with tiny crustaceans called krill that float in it. Baleen whales use their tongues to push water out, but the krill are held in their mouths by rows of stiff plates called baleen. Then, gulp, it's a krill supper! Krill swim in large clusters that provide a hearty meal for these giants. Belugas, orcas, and other toothed whales eat larger sea creatures such as fish, squid, and crabs.

humpback whale and calf

family MATTERS

Since they're mammals, whales give birth to live young and nurse their babies. Blue whales, the largest known animal on the planet, have the largest babies on Earth. These not-so-little ones weigh in at some 6,000 pounds (2,722 kg) and gain about 9 pounds (4 kg) every hour by drinking their mothers' fatty milk. Over time, these baby blues will grow to be as long as two school buses.

65

Minke whale
Length: 26 to 33 feet (8 to 10 m)
Weird but True: Curious minkes sometimes swim alongside ships.

giants
OF THE SEA

Whales come in many different shapes and sizes. There are 71 known species that range from just 5 to more than 100 feet (2 to 31 m) long. Dive into some fascinating facts about these mammoth mammals.

Beluga
Length: 10 to 15 feet (3 to 5 m)
Weird but True: The beluga uses its dorsal (back) ridge to punch breathing holes in Arctic ice.

Blue whale
Length: 75 to 105 feet (22 to 32 m)
Weird but True: Blue whales can weigh up to 200,000 pounds (90,719 kg).

Sperm whale
Length: 36 to 59 feet (11 to 18 m)
Weird but True: The sperm whale can dive to 3,300 feet (1,006 m), deeper than any other large whale.

67

Narwhal
Length: 13 to 15 feet (4 to 5 m)
Weird but True: The male narwhal has a giant tooth on its head.

Narwhals gather in the Arctic Bay off the coast of northern Canada.

Bowhead whale
Length: 38 to 50 feet (12 to 15 m)
Weird but True: Bowhead whales swim under the ice when frightened.

northern right whale and calf

Right whale
Length: 35 to 55 feet (11 to 17 m)
Weird but True: The right whale's huge head can take up a third of its length.

69

DOLPHINS

the need for
SPEED

Ultrasmooth skin, curved fins, and a streamlined body help dolphins slice through the water at speeds of up to 14 miles an hour (23 km/h). Some, like the bottlenose, can even twirl gracefully through the air. Cruising along, this marine mammal surfaces about every ten minutes to suck in air through its blowhole. Even taking a nap doesn't stop the dolphin from coming up for a breath—half of its brain always stays awake, telling the animal when to breathe.

Bottlenose dolphins are social animals, usually swimming in groups of 2 to 15.

mouthy MAMMALS

These social marine mammals are some of the most advanced communicators in the sea. Squeaks, clicks, and chirps alert other dolphins in their group, or pod, to food or a predator lurking close by. Dolphins even send each other messages using body language, such as tail slaps and fin rubs. They also use echolocation to "see" with their ears. Bouncing a series of clicks off other animals or objects, these mammals use the echoes to figure out how far away an object is and which way it is moving. Then whistle, click, whoosh. They're off again.

bottlenose dolphin

A bottlenose dolphin (far left) swims with a pod of Atlantic spotted dolphins.

dolphin "SPEAK"

BEHAVIOR:

- Two dolphins rubbing fins after being apart
- S-shaped body posture
- Approach from behind
- Tail-slapping
- Touching fin to the side of another dolphin

THE DOLPHIN MIGHT BE SAYING:

- Hello! I missed you.
- Watch out!
- Let's play.
- Back off!
- Hey, give me a hand.

Dolphins sleep with one eye open.

73

Spinner
Length: 6 to 7 feet (1.8 to 2.1 m)
Weird but True: Among the most acrobatic dolphins, spinners can twirl in the air four times in a row.

meet the
DOLPHINS

Dolphins and whales are closely related and belong to a group of marine mammals called cetaceans. So when is a dolphin a dolphin? Generally smaller than whales, dolphins often have narrower jaws and always have teeth. Many whales are toothless. Take a look at some of the coolest dolphins in the sea.

Orca
Length: 23 to 32 feet (7 to 9.8 m)
Weird but True: Often called "killer whales," orcas are actually the world's largest dolphins.

Risso's dolphin
Length: 8.5 to
13 feet (2.6 to 4 m)
Weird but True: These
scrappy dolphins can
be covered with scars,
often from rough-
housing with other
Risso's dolphins.

Pacific white-sided
Length: 5.5 to 8 feet (1.7 to 2.5 m)
Weird but True: Like many
dolphins, Pacific white-sided
dolphins like to play with seaweed.

Atlantic spotted
Length: 5 to 7.5 feet (1.6 to 2.3 m)
Weird but True: Atlantic spotted
dolphins get more spots as they age.

OCEAN EXTREMES

and the winner is...

A ll ocean animals are cool in their own way, but these ten creatures are truly incredible.

Fastest Fish:

Sailfish can reach speeds of 68 miles an hour (109 km/h) as they slice through the sea—and leap through the air!

Deepest Dweller:

The deep-sea snailfish, with its bulbous head and partly transparent body, lives five miles (8 km) down in the Pacific's Mariana Trench.

Top Predator:

Great white sharks can reach more than 20 feet (6 m) in length and weigh more than 5,000 pounds (2,268 kg). They have razor-sharp, triangular teeth that can be more than 2.5 inches (6.4 cm) long—which they use to rip chunks off their prey, such as dolphins, seals and sea lions, sea turtles, mollusks, and crustaceans.

Fastest Ocean Animal (without leaping):

If you subtract the airtime from the sailfish's speed, the killer whale is the speediest animal in the water, clocking in at 34.5 miles an hour (56 km/h).

Loudest Creature:
Blue whales' vocalizations can reach 188 decibels—louder than a jet engine—and can be detected more than 500 miles (800 km) away.

Biggest Invertebrate:
Giant squid can grow up to 43 feet (13 m) in length. They also have eyes the size of a human head—the largest in the marine kingdom.

Smallest Fish:
Australia's stout infantfish is less than an inch (2.5 cm) long when it finishes growing.

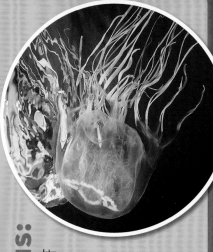

Most Venomous:
Just one sea wasp—a kind of jellyfish with 60 tentacles, each of which can grow up to 100 feet (30 m) long—has enough venom to kill 60 adult humans.

Biggest Beast:
Blue whales are the largest animals that have ever lived—on land or sea. Females are slightly larger than males and can grow to be 79 to 89 feet (24 to 34 m) and weigh more than 100 tons (91 t). The heaviest blue whale known weighed more than 190 tons (172 t).

Longest Migration:
Arctic terns migrate back and forth from Greenland to the Antarctic—about 44,000 miles (71,000 km) total—every year. In the water, gray whales travel the farthest, migrating up to 13,000 miles (35,406 km) round-trip each year.

MARINE REPTILES

Tough, waterproof skin is marine reptiles' best asset when they are below the waves. It keeps them in a high position on the food chain because they're awfully tough to chomp and chew. But they have other great features that help them survive in their watery world, like special glands to get rid of all the salt they drink. Check out these highly adapted, water-loving reptiles.

SEA TURTLES

home sweet home—
EVERY TWO YEARS

Heaving herself from the surf, a female green sea turtle grunts as she slides her 350-pound (159-kg) body across a sandy beach. She comes home to nest every two years, perhaps traveling thousands of miles to return to the beach where she was born. No one knows exactly how she finds her way, but she may rely on Earth's magnetic fields for her finely tuned sense of direction. Finding a spot on the beach, she scoops out a hole with her rear flippers, laying 80 to 150 eggs, and then covers her nest with sand. She'll return to the same beach about every two weeks for the next few months to lay more eggs and then cover them with sand. When her nesting duties are done, she will shuffle back to the sea and won't look back even once.

female green sea turtle heading into the ocean

hawksbill turtle eggs

green sea turtle

Sea turtles can't pull their heads and limbs into their shells like land turtles can.

baby leatherback
sea turtle

baby olive
ridley sea turtles

MARCH to the sea

About two months after a mother sea turtle lays her eggs, baby sea turtles nose their way out of their shells, digging for a whole day to reach the sand's surface. The babies' flippers quickly grip, push, grip, push as they race to the sea. Only one out of every thousand eggs laid by female sea turtles will survive to become an adult. Here's why:

- 1,000 eggs are laid, buried on sandy beaches.

- 800 sea turtles hatch. The rest never fully develop.

- 400 make it off the beach into the open ocean.

- Others are eaten by crabs, birds, and fish.

- 200 survive two to five years at sea. The rest are eaten by predators or get caught in fishing gear.

- One lives to be 30 to 70 years old. The remaining sea turtles fall victim to sharks, capture, and disease.

Note: These numbers are approximate.

baby loggerhead
turtle

81

MARINE IGUANAS

Male marine iguanas **butt heads** for up to **five hours** when **battling** over **females.**

seafaring LIZARD

Swishing from side to side, flat tail floating behind, a marine iguana swims through tropical waters and tidal pools. These are the only seagoing lizards on the planet. Every few minutes, a marine iguana's bulbous, rocklike snout shoots above the surface because it needs to breathe. This creature swallows a lot of salt water while chomping down on its algae meals. But its body has a way to get rid of the salt it doesn't need. A special gland near its eyes collects the salt and when the lizard is back on land, *aaah-chooo!* It sneezes out the salty stuff in a burst of tiny flakes. Drifting down like snow, the flakes cling to its bumpy head like a funny-looking wig.

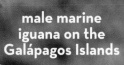

male marine iguana on the Galápagos Islands

foot of a marine iguana

A marine iguana eats algae near the Galápagos Islands.

accordion-like
ADAPTERS

Coming ashore for a rest or a good meal, these lizards use their long, sharp claws to grab on tight to rocks as they munch seaweed and scrape algae off the rocks with their sharp teeth. When food is scarce for months, marine iguanas not only get skinnier but also shorter. Their spines actually shrink and then expand again when the animals can find more seaweed treats.

SALTWATER CROCODILES

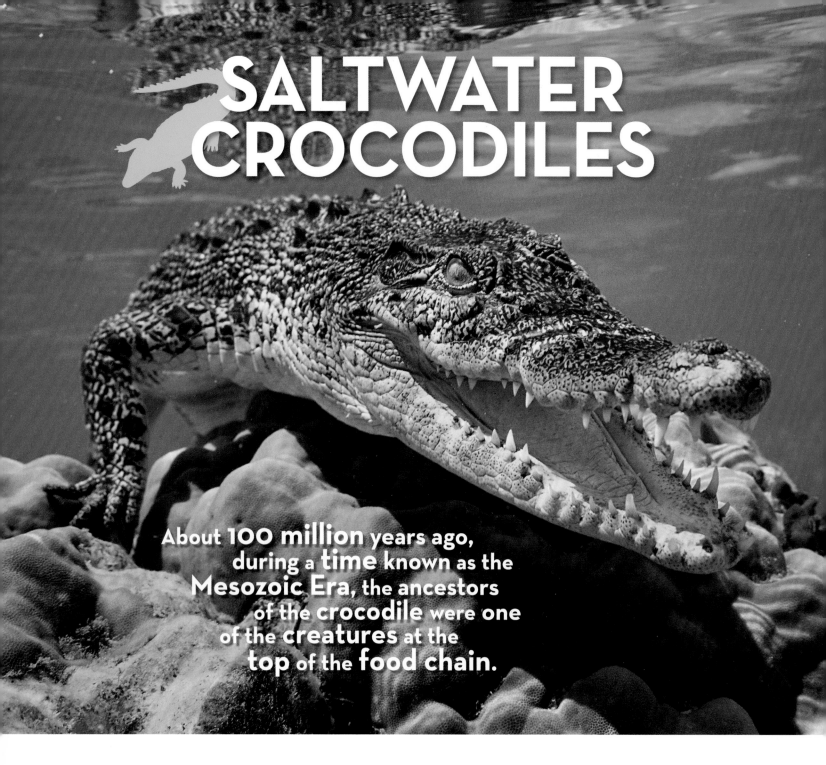

About **100 million** years ago, during a **time** known as the **Mesozoic Era,** the ancestors of the **crocodile** were **one** of the **creatures** at the **top** of the **food chain.**

EYES AS BIG as their (two) stomachs

These carnivores munch mostly on small mammals, birds, fish, crabs, insects, and frogs, but they will eat dead animals and carcasses, too. They can't chew—instead, saltwater crocodiles chomp down with their massive jaws, crush their prey, and then swallow it whole. Their jaws are so strong, they can chomp with 5,000 pounds (2,268 kg) of pressure per square inch. Though they don't use their teeth to eat, crocs do use their teeth to kill prey. When they lose a tooth, it is replaced almost immediately. These carnivores can go through as many as 8,000 teeth in their lifetime. Saltwater crocodiles have very acidic stomachs that break down their food. They also swallow small rocks to help them digest their food. But every time a saltwater crocodile opens wide, it isn't to take a bite. It also opens its mouth to keep cool. This process is called mouth gaping and is similar to how a dog pants.

saltwater crocodile showing its many sharp teeth

SALTWATER CROCODILE VS. ALLIGATOR:

These reptile relatives can be hard to keep straight—especially when they're halfway submerged! But only the saltwater crocodile can live in brackish, or salty, water; alligators (and other crocs) can only survive in freshwater. Here are some other clues to tell the two species apart.

SALTWATER CROCODILE:

- Longer, thinner snout
- Lighter skin
- V-shaped jaw
- Two long teeth on lower jaw visible when mouth is closed
- Carries young to the water, then leaves them on their own
- Has salt glands on its tongue so it can live in salt water

ALLIGATOR:

- Shorter, wider snout
- Darker skin
- U-shaped jaw
- No visible teeth on lower jaw when mouth is closed
- Stays with young after carrying them to the water
- Doesn't have salt glands on its tongue

saltwater crocodile

alligator

MARINE BIRDS

Though they nest on land, marine birds have large, strong wings that help them cover long distances and glide on ocean winds in search of food among the waves. When these feathered hunters spy delectable-looking fish, they dive-bomb to the surface at high speeds. Penguins, on the other hand, are marine birds that can't fly. They dive into the ocean to scoop up their next meal. Jump in for a closer look at these amazing aquatic acrobats.

emperor penguin chicks in Antarctica

PENGUINS

Gentoo penguins go to the sea.

king penguins

tiny
TORPEDOES

Most penguins live on the icy land of Antarctica, near frigid waters topped by thick sea ice. They can't fly, so instead penguins waddle and slide on their bellies across the ice to reach the ocean. When they finally plunge into the water, they become like torpedoes, zooming up to 22 miles an hour (35 km/h) to capture fish and squid and to dodge predators such as seals and orcas. Penguins can swim nine times faster than they can waddle.

Adélie
Height: about 2 feet (0.6 m)
Weird but True: These penguins sometimes swipe stones from their neighbors' nests to line their own.

Rockhopper
Height: about 2 feet (0.6 m)
Weird but True: Rockhoppers are known for their crazy hairdos and for jumping from rock to rock.

Chinstrap
Height: 2 to 2.5 feet (0.6 to 0.8 m)
Weird but True: Chinstrap penguins can dive more than 100 feet (31 m) under the water.

Gentoo
Height: 2 to 2.5 feet (1 m)
Weird but True: Gentoos have long, stiff tail feathers that stick out behind them when they walk.

wacky ways
OF PENGUINS

Spiky feathers, striped faces, yellow chests—their funny "costumes" aren't the only surprising things about penguins.

King
Height: about 3 feet (1 m)
Weird but True: Kings are the second largest penguins after emperors.

89

Royal tern

Young royal terns leave their nests within a day of hatching, then gather with other newly born birds in groups called crèches that can have thousands of royal terns at a time. But they're not totally on their own: At feeding time, parents find their chicks by listening for their unique calls.

marine **BIRDS**

Although they fly the skies to get around, marine birds come to the sea to find their food and have a meal. Get a closer look at some water-bound birds that call both sky and sea home.

royal terns

A royal tern flies in the Gulf of California.

Australian pelican
With a pouched bill that can be up to 1.5 feet (0.5 m) long, these massive seabirds can fly for hundreds of miles in search of a mouthful of fish.

Australian pelican in New South Wales, Australia

Australasian gannet

Australasian gannets fly in large flocks that swoop together down to the ocean surface to hunt fish. When a fish is in sight, a gannet folds its wings back and rockets into a dive, using its serrated beak to grab prey, which is swallowed whole.

Australasian gannets in New Zealand

Atlantic puffin

Bright-beaked Atlantic puffins spend most of their lives at sea, sometimes even resting on the waves, but they build their twig nests high up on cliffs near the water.

Atlantic puffins

Blue-footed booby
Blue-footed boobies show off their feet to prospective mates. The bluer their feet, the more attractive they are to females.

Blue-footed boobies stand above a group of nests on the Galápagos Islands.

BIZARRE
CREATURES OF THE DEEP

Pitch-black and just a few degrees above freezing, the ocean bottom is a harsh place to live, and the fish that survive in these extreme conditions have developed some strange adaptations. Most of these deep-sea residents are bioluminescent, which means chemicals inside their often see-through bodies glow like underwater night-lights. Sporting gargantuan mouths and spiky fangs, some have stretchy stomachs made for catching any meal that happens to fall their way.

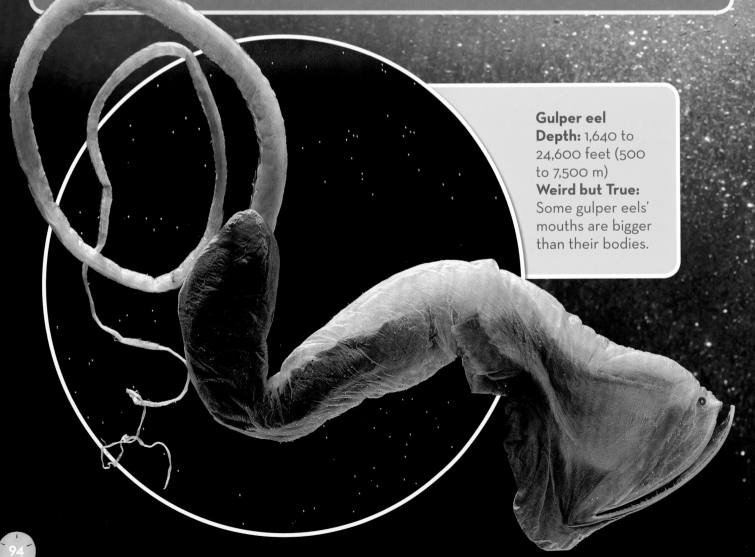

Gulper eel
Depth: 1,640 to 24,600 feet (500 to 7,500 m)
Weird but True: Some gulper eels' mouths are bigger than their bodies.

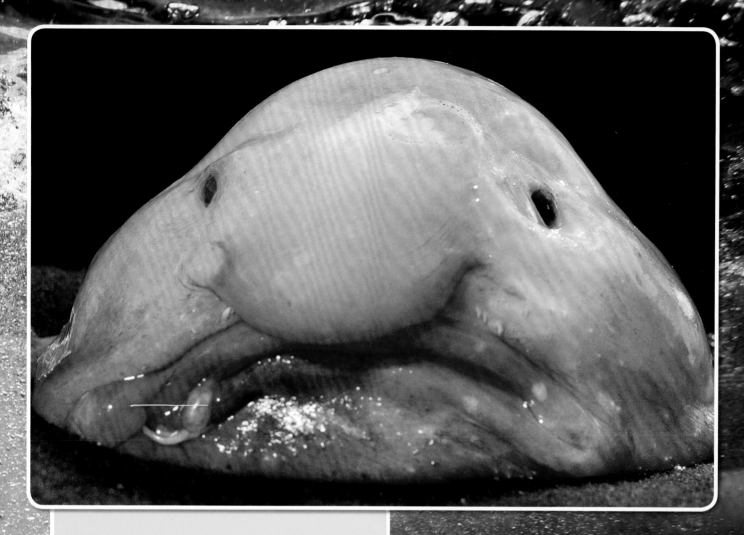

Blobfish
Depth: 2,000 to 4,000 feet (600 to 1,200 m)
Weird but True: Instead of chasing prey, a blobfish may just open its oversize mouth and let food fall in.

Elsman's whipnose
Depth: 0 to 16,400 feet (0 to 5,000 m)
Weird but True: Females can be 15 inches (38 cm) long; males are less than an inch (2.2 cm) long.

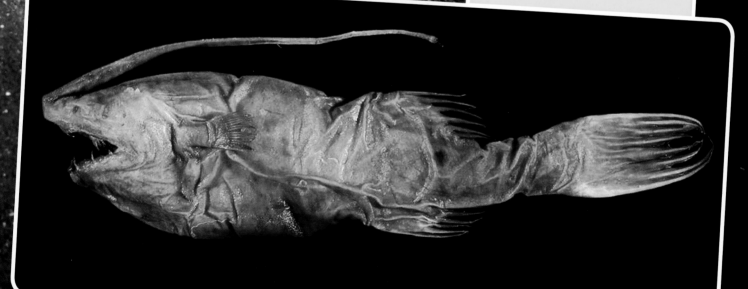

Barreleye fish
Depth: 2,000 to 2,600 feet (610 to 793 m)
Weird but True: This fish has green, tube-shaped eyes and a see-through dome on its head.

Hatchetfish
Depth: 1,310 to 4,130 feet (399 to 1,259 m)
Weird but True: The hatchetfish emits blue light that matches dim sunlight filtering through the water—a form of camouflage called counterillumination.

Deep-sea anglerfish
Depth: 2,600 to 5,280 feet (793 to 1,609 m)
Weird but True: The female has a glowing dorsal fin that acts as a fishing rod and lure.

OCEAN
HABITATS

Since oceans fill Earth from the frigid Poles to the sultry Equator, there are many types of ocean habitats. From watery forests to ice-filled waves, here's a close-up look at a few.

giant kelp forest

underwater
FOREST

Giant, swaying forests of kelp, a type of algae, grow in cool coastal waters and reach up to 200 feet (61 m) tall—the height of a 20-story building! The algae's holdfasts, or rootlike structures, grip the ocean floor, while gas-filled pockets, called bladders, keep the kelp upright as it stretches toward the sunlight. In the waters of the North Pacific, off the coast of places such as California and Alaska, sea otters often make their homes in kelp forests. By wrapping themselves and their babies in kelp that floats on the water's surface, these animals anchor themselves so they can snooze without drifting out to sea. Thousands of other animals rely on kelp forests, too. Sponges, sea urchins, seals, and even orcas hide, hunt, and eat in the towering blades of green.

California
sea lions

ancient ICEBERGS

When Antarctic penguins need a break from fishing, they often chill out on giant, floating chunks of ice called icebergs. These frozen mounds start out as parts of glaciers—massive formations of compressed ice and snow that can be hundreds of thousands of years old. When the edge of one of these slow-moving rivers of ice hits the ocean, it unleashes thunderous groans and rumbles that can be heard miles (km) away. Then chunks of ice, some as tall as 16 stories, plunge into the sea. Icebergs are born!

Chinstrap penguins gather on top of an iceberg.

the GALÁPAGOS islands

Santiago Island in the Galápagos

Strong ocean currents swirl around the Galápagos Islands, off the coast of Ecuador, South America. On the shore, tidal pools sit at the feet of volcanic rock and rough boulders. Chilly waters surround the entire archipelago. Straddling the Equator, the Galápagos are home to animals found nowhere else in the world, including marine iguanas, giant tortoises that can live to be more than a hundred years old, and flightless cormorants, some of the rarest birds in the world.

MANGROVES

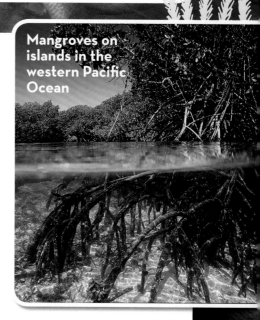

Mangroves on islands in the western Pacific Ocean

Mangrove trees, which grow in tropical waters, are an ideal rest stop for manatees and home to many other animals. A jumble of skinny roots and low-hanging branches, mangroves thrive in estuaries, where fresh water and salt water mix. Oysters and barnacles anchor themselves to the trees' dense roots, helping filter water and trap nutrients in the woody stems. The result is a nutrient-packed nursery for young fish, sharks, crustaceans, and shellfish. Mangroves also provide nesting and hunting areas for seabirds.

PRISTINE SEAS PROJECT

National Geographic Explorer-in-Residence Dr. Enric Sala created the Pristine Seas project to find, survey, and help protect the last wild places in the ocean. His idea is to help preserve these places so they'll be around for a long time. "We have the rare opportunity, right now, to protect many of the most pristine seas around the world," he says. The team is also helping restore areas that have already been damaged by humans.

Dr. Enric Sala

Colorful fish swim over a coral reef.

Golden jellyfish swim in Palau's Jellyfish Lake.

a group of Atlantic spotted dolphins

what they're DOING

The Pristine Seas team is creating marine protected areas, or special places in the ocean designated to help protect and restore ocean life and habitats, a lot like the way that national parks protect wildlife and habitats on land. They're also helping rebuild fish populations that have been overfished for dinner tables and are working to combat pollution and help guard against the effects of climate change.

Moorish idol

Schoolmaster snappers swim through mangrove trees.

20 WAYS
YOU CAN PROTECT THE OCEAN

moon jellyfish

By protecting waterways and conserving water, you can make a big difference when it comes to protecting the planet. These 20 tips help conserve water, keep pollution out of oceans, and protect the animals that live there.

1 Get moving. Bike or walk as much as possible to keep car oil and other chemicals from running off into waterways.

2 Don't release pets such as fish or snakes into rivers, lakes, or the ocean. Nonnative animals can harm an ecosystem.

3 Participate in a beach cleanup.

4 Be a water monitor. Report leaks and drips at home and at school.

5 Take short showers instead of baths. Set a timer to see how clean you can get in five minutes.

6 Never release helium balloons into the air. When they fall into the water, animals can mistake them for food.

7 Make your own soap out of leftover soap slivers to keep pieces of soap from going down the drain—and possibly into waterways. Squish the slivers into cool shapes when they're wet.

8 Avoid using the toilet as a trash can. Flushing things such as medicine may contaminate water sources. It also wastes water.

9 Scoop the poop! Keep your pet's waste from ending up in water sources by cleaning up after your pet and disposing of waste properly.

10 When your family stays at a hotel, reuse towels, washcloths, and sheets.

blue maomao

11 Join a stenciling program with your town or city that paints wacky signs on storm drains. These signs encourage people to keep paint, trash, and soapy water from car washes out of storm drains. This water often flows into lakes, rivers, and oceans.

12 Drink from a reusable water bottle. Disposable bottles take water and other resources to produce.

13 Water your lawn or garden in the early morning. Water doesn't evaporate as fast when the air is cool, so you won't need as much. Save more water by planting native plants adapted to the local environment.

14 Recycle so your trash doesn't end up in water sources.

15 Volunteer at a local aquarium to learn about ocean animals and conservation.

16 Scrape leftovers into the trash instead of rinsing them down the disposal, or make them into compost.

17 Keep your dog on a leash at the beach. Loose dogs can scare or harm creatures that live there.

18 Water is used to produce just about everything, so buy only what you need.

19 Don't feed water animals. They need to find their own food to keep themselves—and their environment—healthy.

20 Share these tips with friends and family.

tropical piranha fish

bottlenose dolphins

The Caribbean reef shark usually prefers shallow waters near the edges of coral reefs, but it has been known to dive to depths of nearly 100 feet (30 m).

GLOSSARY

adapt—to change in order to increase the chances of surviving in a specific environment

Antarctic—the region around the continent of Antarctica

appendage—a body part that is connected to main part of the body

Arctic—the region north of the Arctic Circle

bacteria—tiny, one-celled organisms found in plants, soil, water, air, and animals' bodies

baleen—a hard, comblike material that grows in the upper jaws of baleen whales and is used for filtering plankton from water

bioluminescence—light chemically produced by a living creature

bivalve—an aquatic mollusk with two shells hinged together, such as a clam, oyster, mussel, or scallop

blowhole—a nostril on the top of the head of a cetacean, such as a whale or dolphin

camouflage—colors or patterns on an animal's body that help it blend in with its surroundings

carnivore—an animal that eats other animals

cephalopods—a group of marine mollusks, including squid and octopuses, that have several arms and suckers on their arms and squirt ink for self-defense

cetaceans—a group of marine mammals, including whales and dolphins

coral reef—a rocky ridge of coral shells built up over years as the coral animals inside die

crustacean—an animal with a hard outer shell, joined body, and legs that lives in water, such as a crab, lobster, or shrimp

current—a distinct stream of water that flows within an ocean

cyclone feeding—a process of feeding during which manta rays circle around and around

food chain—the order in which one organism eats another in an ecosystem

hydrothermal vents—areas in the seafloor where magma-heated water shoots up into the freezing-cold seawater around it

iceberg—a drifting mass of ice broken off from an ice sheet or glacier

jet propulsion—when an animal, such as a squid or octopus, squirts a jet of water from its body to propel the animal forward

kelp—a type of seaweed that grows extremely tall in coastal waters

krill—a tiny, shrimplike creature that forms the basis of the diet of baleen whales

magma—molten rock under Earth's crust

mammals—warm-blooded animals that breathe air and have fur or hair; they usually give birth to live young that they nurse

Mariana Trench—a long, narrow valley in the Pacific Ocean that contains the deepest point in the ocean, some 35,827 feet (10,972 m) under the surface

marine—of or relating to the ocean

Mid-Atlantic Ridge—a 6,214-mile (10,000-km)-long mountain range under the ocean

midnight zone—the layer of the ocean from 3,300 feet (1,006 m) down to the bottom of the ocean, where there is no sunlight

mollusks—a group of soft-bodied animals that lack a backbone, are not divided into segments, and are sometimes covered in hard shells, such as clams, mussels, and oysters

pinniped—a marine mammal, such as a walrus, seal, or sea lion, that has four flippers as limbs

plankton—tiny plants and animals that are food for many ocean animals

polyp—an individual coral that builds a limestone shell around itself for protection; also a young jellyfish that has a mouth surrounded by tentacles

predator—an animal that hunts or kills another animal for food

prey—an animal that is hunted or killed by another animal for food

ROV (remotely operated vehicle)—an unmanned, underwater vehicle for ocean exploration that humans operate by remote control

scavenge—to feed on dead animals

submersible—a manned underwater vehicle used for ocean exploration that is built to travel to great depths

sunlight zone—the layer of the ocean from the surface to 328 feet (100 m), where there is abundant sunlight

tentacle—a long, flexible extension, usually on the head or mouth of an animal, used by the animal to touch or grab

twilight zone—the layer of the ocean from 328 to 3,300 feet (100 m to 1,006 m) deep, where there is little sunlight

venom—poison transmitted to other animals by biting or stinging

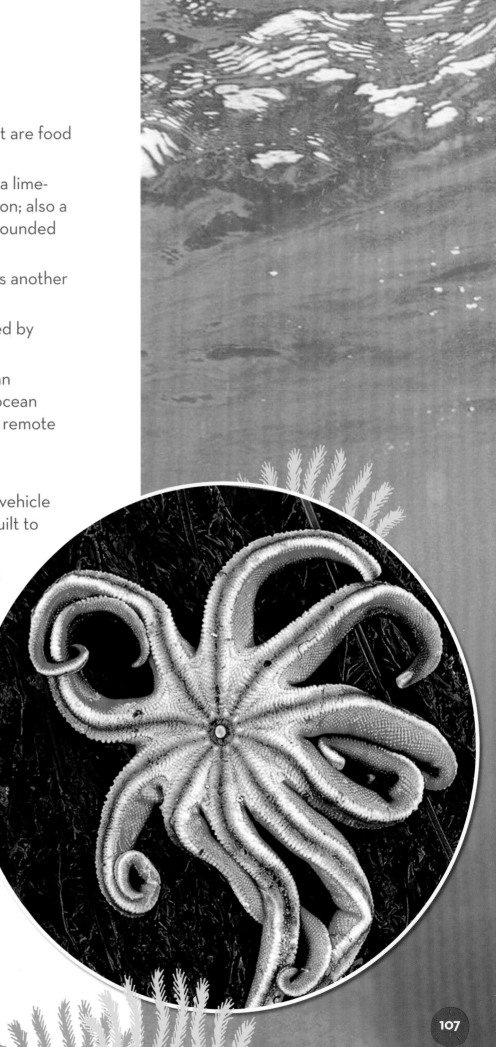

INDEX

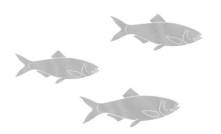

CREDITS

Emperor penguins

ACKNOWLEDGMENTS

FOR CASEY, A TRUE FOUR-LEGGED FRIEND I WAS VERY
LUCKY TO HAVE IN MY LIFE. –J.R.

Louise Allcock, Ph.D., *Martin Ryan Marine Science Institute*
Gisella Caccone, Ph.D., *Yale University*
Raymond Carthy, Ph.D., *Florida Cooperative Fish and Wildlife Research Unit, University of Florida*
Allen Collins, Ph.D. and Michael Vecchione, Ph.D., *National Systematics Laboratory, NOAA*
Sylvia A. Earle, *National Geographic Explorer-in-Residence*
Erin Falcone, *Cascadia Research*
Chadwick V. Jay, Ph.D., *U.S. Geological Survey Alaska Science Center*
Karen Jeffries, *Monterey Bay Aquarium*
Marc O. Lammers, Ph.D., *Assistant Researcher, Hawaii Institute of Marine Biology*
Chris Langdon, Ph.D. and Su Sponaugle, Ph.D., *Rosenstiel School of Marine and Atmospheric Science, University of Miami*
Eleanor Lee, *Boersma Lab, University of Washington*
Bruce Mate, Ph.D., *Marine Mammal Institute, Oregon State University*
Andrew Piercy, Ph.D., *Florida Museum of Natural History, University of Florida*
Kevin Raskoff, Ph.D., *Monterey Peninsula College*
Henry Ruhl, Ph.D., *National Oceanography Centre*
Lisa Schlender, *Cascadia Research*
Emily Shroyer, *Woods Hole Oceanographic Institution*
Martin Wikelski, Ph.D., *Princeton University*
James B. Wood, Ph.D., *Director of Education, Aquarium of the Pacific*

Library of Congress Cataloging-in-Publication Data

Rizzo, Johnna.
    Ocean animals : who's who in the deep blue / by Johnna Rizzo ; with an introduction by Sylvia Earle. -- 1st edition.
        pages cm
    Includes bibliographical references and index.
    ISBN 978-1-4263-2506-9 (pbk. : alk. paper) -- ISBN 978-1-4263-2587-8 (library binding : alk. paper)
    1. Marine animals--Juvenile literature. I. Title.
    QL122.2.R59 2016
    591.77--dc23

                    2015024884

Staff for This Book
Ariane Szu-Tu and Angela Modany, *Project Editors*
Callie Broaddus and Jim Hiscott, *Art Directors*
Greg Jackson, *Designer*
Christina Ascani, *Photo Editor*
Debbie Gibbons, *Director of Maps*
Paige Towler, *Editorial Assistant*
Sanjida Rashid and Rachel Kenny, *Design Production Assistants*
Julie Brown, *Ocean Expert Reviewer*
Tammi Colleary-Loach, *Rights Clearance Manager*
Michael Cassady and Mari Robinson, *Rights Clearance Specialists*
Grace Hill, *Managing Editor*
Joan Gossett, *Senior Production Editor*
Lewis R. Bassford, *Production Manager*
Darrick McRae, *Manager, Production Services*
Susan Borke, *Legal and Business Affairs*

The Monterey Bay Aquarium Research Institute videotaped the barreleye fish on page 96 for the first time ever live with an underwater robot.

Published by the National Geographic Society
Gary E. Knell, *President and CEO*
John M. Fahey, *Chairman of the Board*
Melina Gerosa Bellows, *Chief Education Officer*
Declan Moore, *Chief Media Officer*
Hector Sierra, *Senior Vice President and General Manager, Book Division*

Senior Management Team, Kids Publishing and Media Nancy Laties Feresten, *Senior Vice President;* Erica Green, *Vice President, Editorial Director, Kids Books;* Julie Vosburgh Agnone, *Vice President, Operations;* Jennifer Emmett, *Vice President, Content;* Michelle Sullivan, *Vice President, Video and Digital Initiatives;* Eva Absher-Schantz, *Vice President, Visual Identity;* Rachel Buchholz, *Editor and Vice President, NG Kids magazine;* Jay Sumner, *Photo Director;* Hannah August, *Marketing Director;* R. Gary Colbert, *Production Director*

Digital Laura Goertzel, *Manager;* Sara Zeglin, *Senior Producer;* Bianca Bowman, *Assistant Producer;* Natalie Jones, *Senior Product Manager*

The National Geographic Society is one of the world's largest nonprofit scientific and educational organizations. Founded in 1888 to "increase and diffuse geographic knowledge," the Society's mission is to inspire people to care about the planet. It reaches more than 400 million people worldwide each month through its official journal, *National Geographic,* and other magazines; National Geographic Channel; television documentaries; music; radio; films; books; DVDs; maps; exhibitions; live events; school publishing programs; interactive media; and merchandise. National Geographic has funded more than 10,000 scientific research, conservation, and exploration projects and supports an education program promoting geographic literacy.

For more information, please visit nationalgeographic.com, call 1-800-NGS LINE (647-5463), or write to the following address:
National Geographic Society
1145 17th Street N.W.
Washington, D.C. 20036-4688 U.S.A.

Visit us online at nationalgeographic.com/books

For librarians and teachers: ngchildrensbooks.org

More for kids from National Geographic: kids.nationalgeographic.com

For information about special discounts for bulk purchases, please contact National Geographic Books Special Sales: ngspecsales@ngs.org

For rights or permissions inquiries, please contact National Geographic Books Subsidiary Rights: ngbookrights@ngs.org

Printed in China
15/RRDS/1